OTHER VOLUMES OF POETRY BY HENRY LANGHORNE

Four West

Henry Langhorne

Pelican Press Pensacola
Pensacola

Four West
Copyright © 2018 by Henry Langhorne

ISBN   978-0-9911640-6-6

First Edition

Pelican Press Pensacola
www.pelicanpresspensacola.com

Front cover design by Arielle Langhorne

To every teacher I've had in my life…

A teacher affects eternity; he can never tell where his influence stops.
— Henry Adams

It is the supreme art of the teacher to awaken joy in creative expression and knowledge.
— Albert Einstein

I am indebted to my father for living, but to my teacher for living well.
— Alexander the Great

Education is not filling a pail, but the lighting of a fire.
— W. B. Yeats

Better than a thousand days of diligent study is one day with a great teacher.
— Japanese proverb

TABLE OF CONTENTS

TABLE OF CONTENTS....continued

PREFACE

The title of this book is the name of the cardiac and intensive care unit—4 West—where I practiced cardiology. In the book I have selected "doctor poems" written over fifty years of practice as a cardiologist, followed by new poems since my last book. Dealing with death is a common theme throughout the book, but to heed the well-worn cliché: *Write about what you know*, this has been a testimony of my life's work. Many physician-poets share this unique experience. While such poetry can be depressing for readers, it may help them face reality and cope with the inevitable.

My career in medicine has been in part because of a need to belong. I realize this sense of belonging is what most characterizes human nature. Medicine is the art of protecting and sustaining human belonging against the varieties of human suffering. The loss of any part of the body or its use threatens how we play our part; the art of medicine ultimately fails and death prevails.

When medicine leaves us alone, poetry can provide companionship. It cannot help us recover or bring release from grief, but it can give us companionship in grief. When medication and surgery fail the patient, poetry alone may sustain life somehow. Its recognition of the music of life in all its forms can be uplifting and restore a patient's belonging. That music is all around us: the wind in trees as they speak to each other or what the trout thinks in the shallows, even what clouds have seen. Life is always making life as we live and breathe.

Poets hope their work will bring clear images into the hearts of readers and thus be in more intimate company together. It is in the face of what pulls us away from life's fabric that we need such company. This lightens our grief and brings dignity in dying.

Henry Langhorne

Doctor Poems

4 West

I'm tired of walking down this hall
to meet their wives for the last time.

Sometimes I stop and plan my words
as if they were born today.

Looking out of a window at clouds
prompts me to search for softer words.

Time runs out, nurses and chaplain
linger in the doorway to hear

if I've found a different way
to say he's dead.

Half Tones to Jubilee 1988

Car Lot

A new car with warranty
makes life easy for the first two years
or thirty thousand miles.
Then time runs out,

aging organ systems like heart, lung,
brain sputter and misfire,
old body machines
after so many years of effortless living.

They come in rows,
filling the service lines,
seeking new parts.
Some drive away, patched for a while,

others rust on the lot.
There are no bargains with the dealer.
He can recall them anytime—
they were only gifts.

The Pharos 1989

The Gold Coast

They seek the hospital Riviera—
the well-to-do or just well insured
want rooms with thick carpets

and Gauguin copies on the wall.
Some come in wheelchairs
with new Gucci luggage

and nasal oxygen hissing
on their last vacation—
color TVs, cordless phones,

rare filet or fresh flounder
matched with burgundy
or a very dry chablis.

The bathrooms are clean—
the Gideon bibles never opened.
They sit there on the Gold Coast

with an after-dinner tray
of Demerol and Seconal,
looking at the sunset.

Negative Capability 1990

Michael's Gift

Dr. Kirklin's surgical waiting room
is filled every Tuesday afternoon
with transplanted hearts.
Pumps that never missed a beat
since the first trimester
in their mother's womb
return for careful testing.

Dorothy and her three children
are grateful for Michael's gift.
An army of Coxsackie viruses
had invaded her heart last year,
destroying its delicate muscle fibers
and leaving her with a broken pump,
an unfit home for the soul.

Michael was once a track star
and Olympic gold medal winner until
he exploded his brain with a Smith & Wesson
after the drugs and booze ran out.
They packed his heart in an ice chest
and flew it to Dr. Kirklin in Birmingham
where Dorothy waited alone in a motel.

Now at night she puts the children down
and tells them bedtime stories.
After drinking too much wine alone
she lies in bed and feels him pumping
and running beneath her breast.
They sleep together
and in her dreams she runs his race.

Emerald Coast Review 1991

A new heart will I give you, and a new spirit
will I put within you.   — Ezekiel 36:26

Shoeshine Time

A Prose Poem

Fred was pleased when the nurse called that afternoon.
His blood test was normal—another six month's reprieve.
They had told him the bone pain might go away
after irradiation, like fever fades with aspirin.
It didn't, but the doctor told the nurse to tell him
remission was not uncommon. Like dying, he thought
as he drove his Ford pick-up past his cotton field.
It looked struggling and even smaller to old eyes.
He passed his high school that looked so modern,
the kids too well dressed. This was not his time,
Fred decided. Another six months? It was a better hand
than his young Rachel was dealt that winter long ago.

We die, he thought, and we know it all the while
until one day feels different from all the rest,
like noticing a Burger King where Woodfin's mill was,
or tenement houses that had spread like kudzu
across the family cotton land. He shrugged it off.
Then he parked in front of the old Albert hotel
and limped up the stairs. Bennie had been shining shoes
in the lobby since Fred's honeymoon at the Albert
many years ago. He strained up the shine chair
for the very first time, winked at Bennie, and smiled.

Hotel Albert
Selma, Alabama
1995

American Physicians Poetry Association 1998

My Last House Call

He was one of my first patients
back when doctors made house calls
and drank coffee in the kitchen,
so when his wife called me I had to go.

In his room I saw the yellow jaundice
of skin next to his white bathrobe.
The clock was ticking on the mantel
as it would years after.

I wanted to say to him, death will come
as a lover, dancing you and gifting you
with comfort—years of doctoring have left
little room in my pockets to stash tears.

I wrote prescriptions for nausea and pain,
the only comfort I had to offer,
but as I left the room she kissed his cheek,
promised him strawberries in the morning.

The Pharos 2001

Heart Patients I Have Known

I remember a man who wore a toupee,
flashy clothes and gold jewelry—
He died screaming with his eyes shut
and legs kicking at some invisible intruder.

I remember a ninety year old grandmother
who sat up in front of her daughters,
took a deep breath for me as I listened
to her lungs, and left us without a sound.

I remember a farmer who looked at me
with a puzzled face as pain crushed him
like an elephant's foot and he stared
as if he saw someone invisible to me.

I remember the blue-eyed father
of a close friend of mine, found cold
in his bed and hauled to where I waited.
I could not make him warm again.

Wives and children sat in plastic chairs,
stunned and blank as darkened lamps.
There are days when such memories
swarm up and stick like dead flies—

days when they stand in line to speak,
then fall around me like scattered cards.
Their voices disappear, except for
the smallest of sounds, something like a sob.

Journal of the American Medical Association (JAMA)
2003

My Oath

Once I dissected the human body
but could not find the soul.
Later on the wards I watched
the same bodies as a servant
to the dying—pledged by an oath
in a hallowed veil of service.

Five decades of doctoring
have passed—forgotten long ago
the origins and insertions,
the names of muscles and bones—
yet I have been amazed at healings
that would shake any disbelief.

My patients moved from youth
as leaves drift slowly,
then plummet to the ground
in old age. Now I can sit
at ease with the dying—
because of love, of letting go.

Winter Clothes 2003

My Doctor

As we age, my doctor said,
secretions dry up
and do not tickle as they slide
down our throats---
so at unexpected times we lose
our voices to hoarseness.
This is especially bad
on the telephone or trying
to read something
to an audience, like poetry.

According to my doctor
dryness seems to be
the buzz word for so many
of life's problems---
not just the skin, although
mine is constantly shedding
after years of ultraviolet light.
Let's accept dryness for
all mucous membranes
and get on with serious things.

Some say the universe
is drying up and the sun has us
in its cross hairs. We could seek
an amphibious life with toads
in a tropical rain forest, but
clouds keep rising as the heat
pushes them up. Soon we would
become extinct like the golden toad.
My doctor knows his dryness
but has no concept of global warming.

Winter Clothes 2003

11

The Doctor Said

It's simple. When you get old
your skin gets thin
the doctor said
with a look of impatience
as if I should know
there was no other explanation.

Let's hope they find a cure,
the doctor said
as he smiled and shut the door.
Maybe the last word
has already been spoken
and we're just afterthoughts.

You'll just have to wait,
the doctor said
and waiting is such mean time.
Most of us want to say
bring it on, get on with it,
whatever it is.

Winter Clothes 2003

Keeper of Keys

What turns the key
and jump-starts the heart
as the fetus floats in darkness?
After that, regular rhythm
is taken for granted
for so many years until
one day there is rebellion
in the land of hearts—
this four-chambered muscle
stumbles, skips, sputters

like an old Model T Ford
lurching down a busy freeway.
The next keepers of the key
are no mystery—
they are many places,
well known as defibrillators
that shock the quivering heart
and restore normal rhythm.
After their searing jolt
the heart simmers for seconds

like meat on a backyard grill.
Tense witnesses watch a monitor
record no heart beat, only
footprints of a stunned muscle.
But it boots up somehow,
sputters for an anxious moment,
then marches in cadence
as it had since the first impulse
was created long ago
by that mystical keeper of keys.

Winter Clothes 2003

I Have My Dead

I have my dead.
I cannot afford to let them go.
They cheer me up
at other patients' funerals
and remind me
to buckle my seat belt.

When I am brushing my teeth
they will whisper
that the dead of the day
are starting their journey
to some distant place
they always knew they would go.

My dead look down on me
as I lie reading in my bed.
Before I slip under the surface
of a page into the first chapter
of a dream they remind me
to turn out the lamp.

Passenger 2003

Night Call

Sixty-nine years have taught me
we are all amateurs at life,
moth-eaten by selfish needs.
We no longer listen
for evening whippoorwills
or an owl's lonely hoot
from the pines at first dark.

Driving home this morning
while the sun was still sleeping
I left another patient cold
in his bed. After his eyes shut
I wondered if he would be
feeling his way to the hereafter
like a blind spider in a cave.

If only I could hear
voices scuttling in the wind
I might then comprehend
my destiny and go down
into the earth with the hope
that the trumpet of judgment
will call me by my name.

The Pharos 2003

Memorial Service at Noon

Noonday services have always been difficult—
I have to cancel late morning patients,
skip lunch, and make late evening rounds.

His friends stand in line to sign the book
and receive credit for their respect,
then shuffle into pews and grieve in stanzas.
The acoustics make every sound cling like lint.
Is the only hymn they know *Amazing Grace?*

I survey the array of stained glass windows—
beatitudes shine through saints' faces,
their suffering finished, and all their sins
forgiven so they may look down on us,
exuding faith and fortitude.

After the service there will be a reception
but I will slip away after I let the survivors
one at a time thank me for everything.

The Clarity of Last Things 2005

Old Patients

Many he can't recall
but all of them he recognizes
when their dry lips whisper
their presence from the other side—

not really thanks, not accusations
though most seem grateful—
but words of gratitude implied
to be stored in his cluttered bag

of memories with names that awaken him
near dawn, names drawn that quiver
in his mind more like the flutter
of a moth disturbed in daylight.

There are now days
when he realizes he cannot remember
if he last saw them in their rooms
on evening rounds or in his dreams.

Now in his winter years
before sunlight slips through his window
he lies there, free of the fears
each day used to bring him.

Some time later his office door will open
and one will enter, one who will come
to call out his name,
one he had thought was gone.

The Clarity of Last Things 2005

To Stay Visible

In his final days of hospice
he drifts in and out
of morphine slumber while
she reads Hemingway short stories
to him at the bedside
and leaves his desk light on
through the cold winter nights.

In the mornings he smiles
to see her standing over him,
watching his chest rise and fall.
She leaves his desk untouched.
She wants things to stay
that way—his pen and journal,
old cigarette butts on a tray.

He rallies when he sees the lace
on a favorite nightgown
as she leans down to kiss him.
How these two must strive
to stay visible to each other,
never naming what it is
they see that keeps him alive.

Hurricane Review 2006

Big Charity *

She stood like a fortress
on the New Orleans skyline.
We called her *Big Charity*,
her gray walls a haven for the poor.
She taught generations of doctors
the art of diagnosis and treatment,
how to wield a knife,
separate good tissue from bad,
cure the failing heart.
We endured twelve-hour shifts
on her wards, then walked
her halls at night, silent
except for moans from wards
whose beds were always filled.
We slept in scrub suits
without dreams. When we left,
we were changed forever—
not more compassionate
or fearful of death, but resigned
to the fragility of this life.
There would be no emergency
or complication we had not faced.
Thanks to *Big Charity*
we would stand beside the dying,
whisper to each of them
a wordless benediction, and never
shed a tear until we left the room.

* Charity Hospital, New Orleans
1735-2005

As Fate Would Have It 2007

Caught

Intensive Care

fisherman father
tonight you are caught
like brown trout

on the glistening lines
you sailed in Wyoming
their sweet flesh

you still remember
tonight you swim in pain
I give you my answers

though I do not know
how to live with the loss
something you teach me

in a sliver of quiet
gives you also my pain
you swim through it

your grey eyes fasten
on mine and teach me
a lesson I should know

Emerald Coast Review 2007

Like a Whooping Crane

is how they described your murmur.
Students, interns, residents filed by,

stethoscopes draped around their necks
like beads, to listen to the whooping sound

of a leaking valve, the cry of a white crane
trapped in your heart chambers.

They had to split your breastbone
with a saw to let it out and stitch in

 a new valve, its metal discs clicking
and clapping while they sewed your chest

and wired you shut. No one remembers
how and when it left the operating room.

That night, outside your CCU window,
a full moon shone down on the bay

where a large, white crane stood at last,
roosting in quiet, shallow water.

The Hurricane Review 2007

Sentinel Node

For my wife

You are the guardian of the gate.
All caravans must face you first.
How do you recognize malignant ones?
The ductal from the lobular legions?
Easy, you say—the first come

grouped in force—the others sneak,
in single file like marauders
on the trail of some wagon train.
You are tested with dye to learn
how strong your fortress is.

This invasion was cowardly,
without declaration of war.
Your hostess must face decisions.
She has begun to see herself as part
of another life larger than her own.

The Pharos
Winter 2007

Atrial Fibrillation

I knew you would come again.
Years ago the doctors said
it was too much wine
at Christmas time---
"the holiday heart."
Blood thinners and electric shock
drove you away,
my heart beat again
in effortless synchrony.
But early morning today
you returned, pounding
your chaotic rhythm in my ear.

The Pharos
2008

Hands and Images

My bishop covered my twelve-year-old head
with his ringed hand and confirmed me.
Priests offer their hands in benedictions,
to bless a union, or even heal the sick.
A lover's caress can work wonders.

Centuries ago physicians learned the trade—
palpating for lymph nodes, tumors,
swollen livers and spleens,
even invading the most private parts
with probing gloved hands.

Now we doctors use our hands
to guide catheters into arteries and veins,
or move an ultrasound transducer
over the body, producing images,
brightly colored and cold.

The Hurricane Review 2009

A DeFuniak Farmer

Alonzo was a Florida Panhandle farmer—
a patient who never missed an appointment,
heart scarred and blood sugar too high,
who suppressed aging with the joy of simple life.

He had spent his years working the earth—
his crops gave nourishment to his spirit
which bore the weight of seventy-odd years.
I remember his wrinkled, sunbaked face,
his toothless smile, and how he proudly spoke
of two grandchildren and the two little farms
he had worked to give to them someday.

When he did not return in the spring,
in his starched denim shirt and faded overalls
bearing gifts of peanuts and corn,
I had to leave as they filed his chart away.

In the Country of Rain 2009

Morning Report

Intensive Care Waiting Room

A family member struggles with his pillow
as morning strains to pump daylight
through the tinted windows of the waiting room.
His elbows ache on wooden chair arms,
yesterday's newspaper crumpled in his lap.

Like yesterday, doctors will emerge
through the swinging doors, one by one
to reveal what has happened through the night.
Some in the waiting room will hold back tears,
others will utter groans of relief.

He rises slowly, his back stiffened,
unsteady at first on his numbed feet.
There will be no cafeteria breakfast for him
until his turn comes to hear the morning report.
Black coffee has become a regular diet.

Elevators open outside as the night shift leaves.
Standing alone across the disheveled room
he grips a plastic cup and fills it with coffee,
as dark and as hard for him to stomach
as the moment before him.

In the Country of Rain   2009

In Medical School

We dissected human bodies
but did not find their souls.
Later, on the wards
we found the same bodies
lying in muck
with eternity close by—
fragile lives,
some like a dollhouse
crushed by wheels of science
driven by good and bad doctors.

Four decades later,
the bodies have not changed.
They wonder, as I,
if we are to die in the earth
or live in perpetual clouds.
They have no time left
to grasp anything of their lives—
nor do I grasp it,
wrapped all these years
in a hallowed veil of service,
pledged by oath
to be someone so different
from what I used to be—
a servant to the dying.

In the Country of Rain 2009

His Fluttering Heart

"My heart is fluttering," he told me
on his first office visit, dwindling at age 85.
I checked him over and gave him some pills.

Some months later it was found
that he was anemic and needed blood.
Colon cancer had riddled his liver like a dartboard.

Oncology told him they had nothing more to offer.
As they closed the door they mentioned Hospice
but he came back to see me again.

With a smile on his pale, gaunt face
he thanked me and said he wanted me to know
that his heart didn't flutter anymore.

In the Country of Rain 2009

A Doctor's Remedy

The long day of doctoring finally ends.
To forget the silence of a lifeless room,
the looks of despair waiting in hospital halls,
it sometimes takes a very dry martini.

It stands not just as a panacea or a cure-all,
and surely not as a potential risk of addiction,
but as a calculated blend of gin or vodka with
vermouth, chilled and served straight up with
olive.

It was the favorite drink of Winston Churchill,
Franklin Roosevelt, and many famous writers.
H. L. Mencken once proclaimed the martini to be
"an American invention as perfect as a sonnet."

One could say it has stood the test of time,
a precise mixture guaranteed to please.
Yet because of its proven potency (and concern
for the doctor's health), one should suffice.

In the Country of Rain 2009

Post Chemo Treat

For Patsy

Home again after chemotherapy—
low white blood count
and anemia
mandate solitude
and no virus exposure,
so she curls up
in a mohair throw
on her American Sheraton sofa
and reads a favorite,
Henry James,
fortified
with a bowl of popcorn
and a glass
of chardonnay.

The Pharos 2010

The Vindicated Appendage

They tell you it really shouldn't be there,
like your little toe or an extra finger,
yet it awakens in your seventh decade
like some ancient sleeping volcano
to erupt and spread pus like lava everywhere
in your swollen and painful abdomen.

You find the glare of operating room lights
a comfort—the surgeon swears he will do
most of the work (and not the eager intern).
He then carves through layers and finds
the swollen appendage, the evolutionary baggage.

Later your surgeon tells you Darwin thought
it a vestigial structure, perhaps used
by early primates to digest leaves, but now
scientists believe it may have immune function
of benefit to the body, and even serve
as a haven for useful bacteria to fight infection.

So even if you still itch from morphine
and go home sore, reassure yourself you are
a little brighter as well as a few grams lighter.

The Lay of the Land 2011

31

My Cousin's Fatal CVA *

I wonder, Emily, what you must have felt
the moment of your accident (as it's called),
when you were dealt that losing hand
while fixing breakfast in the kitchen.

In the moment it took millions of neurons
to blow their fuses, a cerebral bleed engulfed
all you'd ever thought or done,
everything you ever knew and loved.

Had your pupils, fixed and dilated,
watched your ill-fated spirit leave the room?
It was so sudden you probably felt nothing,
fear and pain known only to the living.

* (Cerebrovascular Accident)

The Hurricane Review 2011

The Ornamental Stethoscope

After Laennec invented the stethoscope
it became a symbol of our profession:
a Rappaport-Sprague or Littmann model
were cherished icons in our possession.

We carried them neatly tucked away
In white coat pockets on hospital rounds,
to fondle them carefully as we listened
to murmurs, gallops, and heart sounds.

Today many doctors carry stethoscopes
wrapped around their necks for show,
only as ornaments since echocardiograms
tell them everything they need to know.

The Canebrake Collection 2013

Stroke

To Mother

First the good news—
ischemic,
not hemorrhagic—
which means a clot,
not a bleed
caused her stroke.

The treatment?
A "clot buster" drug
to open the vessel
so that her left side
can move again.

Then she sleeps—
left side flaccid.
Hours pass.
The sun sets
and the sun rises.
My mother wakes
and asks me if
she missed breakfast.

November 1995

The Canebrake Collection 2013

Your Inner Ear Concussion

For my wife

When you tripped and hit your head
      on the marble floor
            your blue eyes quivered
      and you lost your balance
as the room whirled about you.
      The doctor called it a concussion
            of the labyrinth (we called it vertigo)
      and prescribed eye exercises.
You cautiously crawled in bed
            and lay back on the pillow
            which became a cloud around you.
Patiently you turned your head
            from side to side.
      The intricate network of your inner ear
      had been jolted out of synch.
We hoped the room would soon stop
            circling your body
              like some giant bird
and land on the blankets,
            enfolding you with its white wings,
              holding you still.

The Canebrake Collection 2013

Congestive Heart Failure

As he struggles upright
on a moon-white sheet,
lungs flooded

by wave after wave,
he sinks under,
then surfaces,

craving the sterile air
with each thrust
of his ribs.

Outside, rain pounds
against the windows,
filling the streets—

water everywhere,
and it is so hard—
so hard to breathe.

Coronary Care Unit
Pensacola 1967

The Canebrake Collection 2013

36

The Thrill

In medical school my first patient
on the pediatric ward was a little boy
dying of rheumatic heart disease.
With stethoscope I learned to hear
the loud murmur in my ear
and how to feel the " thrill " of it.

Our instructor had taught us
how one could feel the pulsation
by placing the palm on the chest wall.
As I did this, his heart leapt up
to meet me, quivering against my palm,
a hummingbird fluttering in harm,

pressed against the cage of his ribs.
He would not be my only patient to die,
but he would always be the first.
Part of me still lingers there,
my hand pressed to his heaving chest
like a promised yet futile request.

When I finally left his bedside
to read the chart at the nurses' station,
the intern had written in his Progress Notes
that the child was "decompensating,"
a term to be perpetuated by others who
preferred it to the fate they knew.

Much later after years of practice
I became aware that most doctors
never say that patients are dying—
perhaps because we cannot accept failure,
because in some way we are cowards,
because we know our hearts betray us.

The Canebrake Collection 2013

Jump-Start

The same energy that jump-started my heart
when I was a five week old fetus in a yolk sac
rescued me again today as I lay
anesthetized in an emergency room,
heart muscle quivering in chaotic rhythm.

My old friend, atrial fibrillation ,had paid me
another visit, not like that Christmas time
when his present was the "holiday heart"
after too much wine, but a greeting
he now lavishes upon many of old age.

My doctor advised electrical cardioversion—
a carefully placed shock to stop the heart
and restore normal rhythm again.
I pondered: Consent to be electrocuted?
Could I know for sure it would start again?

I have no memory of my dreamless sleep
but it may have been like the calm of that fetus
drifting in the warm sea of the womb's nest—
who suddenly came alive when that energy
ignited his heart--as today it reignited mine.

His Doctor Explains His Mini-Stroke

When you could not turn on the computer
and whatever you were doing
or wherever you were ten minutes before
was missing from your mind,
don't you have to wonder what was happening
and why you could not speak to your wife
who was reading the paper across the room?
She told me you had dropped the browser
in your lap and could not pick it up
with your right hand which was drooping
from the arm of your desk chair.

Then your speech returned from wherever
it had traveled with your last thought,
and you blurted out your wife's name.
You again knew the day of the week,
even the president's name, and insisted
you felt as normal as before it had happened.
Then you refused to go to the ER
and repeated a question to your wife
for the third time, she told you
before she hurried from the room.
You had no concern that anything was wrong
as she called me and dialed 911 in the kitchen.

The Canebrake Collection 2013

Stone Bench

Outside a pediatric ward
March rain pelts azaleas in full bloom.
There is beauty in the brevity of flowers—

the toil, the hours put in them.
A mother who just lost a child
understands the death of flowers.

She sits on a stone bench
as if the seat, wide enough for one,
knows grieving must be done alone.

In Search of Solitude 2015

On Evening Rounds

The Emergency Room doctor told me
one of my old patients was dying there.
I remember a heart attack not long
after his wife of sixty years had died.
Now I see an old man who sits speechless
in a chair, rubbing his head with a hand
tethered now to a withering body
like others I have seen on evening rounds.

Without examining him or the labs
I feel cancer lurks in his feeble frame.
Yet, if I sit there for the half hour
I don't have and listen to the story
of a man consumed by a depression
that has drained him as cancer never could,
I might understand how rubbing his head
might serve to soothe the torment he endures—
the ruthless malignancy of his mind.

All the drugs and tests I could imagine
would do nothing to help this grieving man
who can only sit there and rub his head,
perhaps the only way he has to soothe his soul.
As if he knows his life is near its end
the rubbing stops as he gains nourishment
from my presence, and then there is calm.

Christmas Eve 2014

In Search of Solitude 2015

Sanctuary

For fifty years he has been my patient,
all those days not even past.

We've worked together in my office,
on the wards and in intensive care

to survive flu epidemics,
deal with his high blood pressure

and cholesterol, a daughter's divorce,
and a grandchild's autism,

his wife's cancer, his heart attack—
We've lived the panorama of his life

as if we were one person.
We've had our privacy alone together,

detached in a refuge of peace,
our haven from a troubled world.

In Search of Solitude 2015

The Imperfect Door

She had been told she had a murmur,
a defect of her mitral valve
that produced the click and high-pitched sound
I found with my stethoscope,
known by clinicians as mitral prolapse
and confirmed by ultrasound,
the gold standard of this century.

I drew diagrams of the four heart valves,
the doors that open and close in synchrony.
Her mitral valve, deep in the left ventricle,
I likened to the sail of a boat
that billows and snaps in the wind.

I tried to reassure her it was mild,
this internal turbulence, no more
than an imperfect perfection of seal,
no more than the failure to close
with conviction the heart's deepest door.

In Search of Solitude 2015

Empty Room

The room is waiting
for its next guest.
It has cheap bedside stands
and lights too dim to read by.
A corner table
features a chipped vase
stuffed with dead carnations.
A small TV screen
is bolted high on the wall.
Plastic privacy curtains
surround a rolling IV pole,
now empty and tilted.
On a cold tubular bed
with unmade sheets
a patient's imprint lingers.

In Search of Solitude 2015

Resuscitation

When his family asks me what more
can be done to keep him from dying,
I want to tell them that death is not
the worse thing, it is just the last thing;

that miracles are stories told in church;
that blind hope is not a recipe for success.
Do they want us to pretend
we can bring him back to them,

strapped to a face mask as he gasps
and wheezes like an old accordion
while we pump our fists against his sternum
to move blood—barely—through his ancient heart?

I can say do not confuse resuscitation
with resurrection since it fails too often.
I can say we should do nothing more to him.
I can say all this—after fifty years of losing to death.

In Search of Solitude 2015

On Morning Rounds

a favorite patient collapses before you
and as you struggle to catch him,
your knees buckle
and you kneel beside him on the floor.
You hold him as part of him dies,
as others who are dying there
but you walk away stronger
for having touched him.

Perhaps it is all they need from you:
to fall a bit
when they begin to fall
and to rise again with them.
Sometimes, it is what you need
to rise again from your own despair,
to remember who you once were,
who you are.

The Sewanee Review
Winter 2016

Mechanical Man

Spread-eagled in full restraints
Donald Bates glares at me,
a plastic tube in his throat
connecting with a Bennett respirator
whose dials dictate his breathing.
The lump under the skin of his chest,
a Medtronic pacemaker
clicking its seventy beats a minute.

Each night they debate their total control
as he struggles to sleep—
the respirator, heaving and sighing
in a *whish thump* voice
challenging him to live without it,
the electronic genius inside his chest
boasting its rule over pump and flow
to every organ needed to survive.

This morning he scribbles
on a clipboard like a third-grade child,
"Why are you doing this to me?"
Outside the CCU his family waits.
I avoid the clichés---they see in my eyes
the news they fear to hear.
In need of solitude I go home
to fix a doorknob in the kitchen.

The Sewanee Review
Winter 2016

Heartstrings

Fifty years of long corridors
to waiting rooms with welded chairs,
bearing news that held each family
like needle, thread, a knot.

Simple explanations were allowed—
a clot, a tear—but assurance was made
that everything was done,
yet the body held its own weak will,
its faulty pump a failure.

A wife who's been otherworldly still,
listens for a word, a gentle pull
on a chain that softens the harsh cry.
For her, the heart must have soft strings.

Light Is Life 2017

Light Is Life

It was sudden—my collapse.
Heart and kidney abruptly on strike
after eighty-odd years of service.
My new home, a coronary care unit,
all lights and shrill alarms, no windows.

Comatose, I was spared the noises
and unforgettable smells, the insult
of tubes seeking to invade every orifice—
my arms and legs bound in restraints,
my skin a bruise of endless needle sticks.

Still unconscious and on a respirator
with a tube down my throat
I dreamed (I guess it was a dream)
I was in my childhood Sunday School room,
my family sitting ahead of me.

It was dark in the room but I could see them.
Each one urged me not to give up,
not to lose sight of the light.
Outside the school window were the graves
of my father and my grandparents.

I kept looking out of the window,
searching for some light in the darkness.
Then I saw a building, all dark
except for a steel pipe running down its side.
A beam of light reflected off the pipe.

This light spread across the graveyard
and into my Sunday School room.
There it overwhelmed the darkness
around me and poured itself into my life.
I would not yet go into that night.

Light Is Life 2017

Respite

On my eighty-fourth birthday
I did not know
I had a rendezvous with death.

Fifty years of doctoring
have taught me
most had some kind of warning.

Our meeting was sudden
as it overwhelmed me
and put my mind to sleep.

Heart, liver, and kidneys failed
and challenged colleagues
to summon their greatest skills.

I felt as I did before I was born.
But then I awoke
and thanked everyone.

Light Is Life 2017

Their Morning Guest

In antiseptic, windowless rooms
I am their morning guest
after wandering so many nights
among the almost dead.

So as not to feel too close
I touch with gloved hands,
palpate what wilts beneath skin.
They do not want me to read

prayers or gospels from holy books.
If someone asks to see results
of all the blood tests, x-rays,
and scans, I will reveal to them

what was hiding in their veins,
show them ghosts captured on film,
bodies in slow surrender.
That's all they want from me.

Light Is Life 2017

My Patient After Bypass Surgery

He awoke alone,
the light dim in his cubicle—
the uninvited guest he told me about

who had squeezed his heart
with big, hot hands
was no longer in the room.

He lay in a bubble of air
so pure he thought of prayer
and distant saints of childhood.

A nurse's mother-face wavered
and danced before his eyes
as she changed his gown.

At the bedside, I listened
to the *whish thump* of an oxygen machine
cycling. and a clock's exaggerated tick.

A net of IV tubes that trembled
like tinsel and twisting silver
fed him, pain doused by needle stick.

Once more, he was free,
friendly hands now holding his heart—
not squeezing it.

My Discharge Summary

After two weeks of critical care
I was transferred to progressive care
which implied to me enough improvement
to begin planning my own discharge.
All uncomfortable tubes had been removed
except for the one in my bladder.

Though I was still lost in time and place
I could swallow when fed
and walk in the hall with an escort
who pulled my IV pole with its bottles
of nutrient fluids and bag of urine.
Even with a walker I staggered, my gown
gaping open, my backside on display.

The days and nights were as jumbled
as my mind, but as I dozed one day
I decided it was time to go home
and open my bed for someone sicker.

This required a discharge summary,
 so as I lay dozing, always dozing,
I dictated my hospital stay
to my daughter as she sat at the bedside:
the course of my illness, test results,
drugs used, and even my interpretation
of my EKG. Discharge diet, activities,
medications, even return visit
were included in this masterpiece.
Only then did I drift into contented sleep

Light Is Life 2017

My Old Patient

My patient, old and fading,
on his last office visit
said to me,
"There is more to life
than staying alive.
Don't rescue me too much. "

On his farm, ten miles out
over rough gravel roads,
he is done with plowing,
spraying, harvesting.

But he is not done
watching the sun sink
below the windbreak
or listening to the nighthawks
above his fields.

I told his children:
Don't make him move to town.
There is more to tragedy
than dying.

In Search of Solitude 2015

The Untreatable Body

An old medical school professor
who taught anatomy told my class
something like this about the body:

No matter which one you get,
you will never be satisfied.
Wherever you go, day after day,

you will carry it with you.
As it ages, you have to bear
the unfaithfulness of skin and bones

for which the few changes
you can make are small and costly.
Someday you will follow

what you have seen others do
who were much like you,
and who, on occasion without

warning, left behind their lump
of skin and bones to remind
everyone of life's imperfections

Light is Life 2017

4 West at the End of the Hall

More often now I wonder
if for me death will be different
from what I have witnessed
in a lifetime of doctoring?

I remember sitting at bedsides
in the sifted light of dawn
with men and women,
all hopes long gone,
organs failed beyond repair,
their faces an empty stare.

It seemed that fears receded
as time grew near,
my care no longer needed.
At the end, the spirit finds
a way to send comfort
to their restless minds.

It all took place on 4 West
at the end of the hall.
I would sit, holding a hand
slowly cooling. That was all.

The Sewanee Review
Winter 2016

New Poems

Morning Rally

Perhaps someone may have said
life was a struggle before it began.
It takes its toll when the sun shines
and everyone is awake to feel it.
At night when the handkerchief
of darkness settles over one's face
a dream is the only way to breathe.
It gives us a second chance to repair
our tragedies of the day now gone
that leave us stripped of courage.
In the morning we rally with coffee
and try again to convince a new day
that we are still indispensible.

Legacy of a Live Oak

A giant live oak fell
on a wind-bruised day
in early spring.
Iconic tree of the Old South,
it may have lived
over four hundred years.

Protector of the forest
and source of shade,
it provided acorns and home
for birds and squirrels.
Yet death does not end
the nature of such trees.
There is life after death,
but it is not eternal.

Its roots and branches
still provide food and shelter
for others living in the forest.
Thus, a downed live oak
may live in death for
as long as it stood in life.

A Nobel Prize Dream

When I awoke I could not understand
why no one ever thought of such a plan
to rid the world of devastating storms.
Hurricanes require warm ocean water
and low pressure centers for thunderstorms
to generate heat and warm air to rise.

I simply created a fleet of ships,
barges bearing nothing but tons of ice
on call 24/7 whenever
a tropical depression developed
in late summer months or early fall,
the birthday time for lethal hurricanes.

My barges converged on the infant storm
chilling the warm water and rising air
as tons of ice were dumped into the sea.
The aborted storms became world-wide news
and no person I knew was surprised
to hear I would receive the Nobel Prize.

Hurricane Irma
September 10, 2017

61

So Much We Wonder

So often we wonder
what forces hold us together—
the glue and resolve
of our being—

how trees talk to each other

how rivers breathe

what the dove knows

what the trout thinks

in the shallows

even what clouds have seen.

There is so much
we don't know
while life is making life
all around us
as it turns again and again.

Lent 2017

Church in the Forties

For The Rev. Raymond Lord

churches were filled

before bells rang in the tower

women in hats and veils

stirred the still air

with funeral parlor fans

men perspired

in dark vested suits

choirs were small

favorite old hymns were sung

sermons set

the shields of war on fire

at the communion rail

knees ached on cool brick

Advice To An Old Couple Alone On Christmas

Don't begrudge your daughter
and grandchildren skiing with in-laws,
your turn will come again next year.
Instead, witness the cold December sun
make shadows of old oak limbs
that creep across the wooden porch
as the light of evening dims.
Gaze at the kitchen sink
stacked with empty cups and glasses.
Stand beside the decorated window
and wonder how the day passes.
Leave wrappings and ribbons on the floor,
the ornamental tree tilted toward the wall.
Stay in pajamas and drink coffee.
Make much of something small.

Christmas Day 2017

Borrowed Time

Funerals have long since replaced
weddings on social calendars.
Burial services have become too familiar,
and "Amazing Grace" doesn't get it anymore.

Where have all the young voices gone,
and the genuine tears of grief?
Friends exchange congratulatory smiles
as they shuffle by in the aisles.

At the end of services they lumber out
into cruel sunlight and a clenched wind
to cluster in retirement home vans.
Some will not come again.

Two men stop on the church steps,
one white headed with a cane,
one bald and leaning on a walker,
their necks bent forward and fixed.

We're lucky to be here, my friend,
the senior survivor exclaims
as he speaks into the other's good ear—
We're all on borrowed time.

Moving

A new life awakens

within a ripened cell

and moves

from its beginning

into the fullness

of its life.

When the journey ends

it moves once more

into the vast beyond

from whence it came.

Long Time Passing

Where have all the churches gone?
Long time passing
Where have all the churches gone?
Long time ago*

Congregations have grown small
many young people stopped attending
some churches have closed
choirs struggle with contemporary hymns
the Gospel is now read
in the middle of the aisle by clergy
who can barely be seen
the Peace is a time for handshaking
and extending greetings across the aisles
instead of waiting for the coffee hour
some clergy use the pulpit
to express personal trendy views
instead of teachings from the scriptures
preaching from the floor and not the pulpit
portrays the rector as not above listeners
yet often not heard or seen
then on occasion some speak of God as She

Where have all the churches gone?
Long time passing
Long time ago

> * *familiar lines from Peter Seeger's music*
> *made popular by Peter, Paul & Mary, 1962*

Slow Readers

It could become a pastime—
watching old friends try to master
the skills of aging
at each level of incapacity.

My seventy-year-old friends think
they have it made,
yet at eighty-five I am a novice
to Cousin Mick at ninety.

Still, we stay busy,
somehow oblivious to antiquity,
passing around a well-worn edition
of *Aging for Dummies.*

His Demented Wife

She sits silently
at their dining room table,
her mind a dark sea,
her thoughts like waves
that cannot reach the shore.
Then she speaks
severely to her husband
who is loved
and revered by all:
I do not know you,
whoever you are,
sitting at the end of my table—
You will have to leave.
What will my neighbors say?
He sits in silence,
stunned in grief
as he raises his wine glass
in a toast to her.
She can only stare
as he lowers his arm,
a tear falling
into his glass,
unnoticed by her.
Then he drinks the wine
and drinks the tear.

Tuscan Rockets

Although crises keep erupting

from the Middle East to North Korea

there is peace across the Tuscan land

as I travel its ancient hills

where endless rows of thin cypress trees

point their daggers to the sky.

The outside world has no escape

from a nuclear disaster

but here in Tuscany cypress rockets

stand ready to lift all to safety

in Michelangelo's final masterpiece.

Siena, April 2017

Escape to Tuscany

World chaos seemed to be everywhere—
time to escape to Tuscany
where the only arguments had been
about leaving the Middle Ages
with its Gothic spires and flying buttresses
for the symmetry of the Renaissance,
its columns, arches, and domes.

The mysterious and ancient Etruscans
had given Tuscany its birth.
Later came the sculpture and art
of the Florentine genius Michelangelo,
the archetypal Renaissance artist
whose David statue and Sistine Chapel
made him one of the greatest of all time.

Siena, a medieval Tuscan city,
where the message of law and order
is still respected and the Etruscan mystery
hides in the shadows, is a resting place
for a traveler to sit in front of the Duomo,
a black and white Romanesque cathedral,
and have a glass of Chianti wine.

Siena, April 2017

Driving to the Infusion Center

I like to drive

on Sunday mornings

the streets are quiet

no need to speed

the lights are patient

forget seat belts

open the windows

enjoy a cloudless blue sky

A Good Dream

Outside, the solemn trees,
each buried in a cloud of leaves,
seem lost in sleep and make him feel

he should lie down and be fitted
to the dark that has come upon him.
He feels there is no place to go,

no reason to keep him captive so
except in the deep and sheepless
pastures of a long sleep.

Then the doors to the closets
of his unhappiness open, and into
his room fly the ghosts of the grief

and gloom he has suffered—
parents, family, best friend gone,
yet among them a voice tells him

they will come back one night
so that he can dream an ending—
a finale that will turn out right.

Backyard Music

In early morning and late afternoon
I have often watched them
talking to each other—
two crepe myrtle, their branches alive

in wind-stirred motion,
their crinkled flowers blooming
in the hot summer
from deep purple to red and white.

Do all trees speak to one another
or only to their kin?
Does maple talk to oak but not to elm?
They seem so sophisticated

the more I watch them bend and sway
to music always there.
We should take time to listen to
the music made by never-sleeping trees.

Illusions and Delusions

We live in a world
of illusions and delusions
nurtured by our genes
and natural selection
through evolution—
the survival of the fittest.

As our gene pool survived,
so did our lusts and addictions—
endless achievements
and material success were vital
to feed our illusions
of how life should be.

We need somehow to recreate
our flawed gene pool,
to pause and look anew
at everything around us:
all that we have ever done
and everyone we love.

Alive at Eighty-Five

Alive at eighty-five,
I added one more birthday—
not a rare day in June
nor a perfect one
as poet James Russell Lowell
so beautifully described
in lines I had to memorize
during long-ago school days.

I did not have dreams
of special meaning,
and my uneasy balance
on standing was nothing new.
That day I could not sense
the slightest change
in body, mind, or spirit,
a gift received with gratitude.

June 2, 2017

Stem Cells

Dormant in the marrow of man

for two hundred thousand years,

given the gift to divide and multiply,

to replenish adult tissue,

to even repair the failing heart,

they can be grown and transformed

into cell types with features

of muscles or nerves,

hence the heart, a four-chambered

muscle, can be repaired

because these stem cells heal

like the Creator's hand

when harvested and implanted

like new seed in old earth.

A Prose Poem on Father's Day

June 18, 2017

Memory is the sense of loss
and loss pulls us after it.
On this Father's Day, my fifty-sixth,
my father had only twelve.
He was also short-changed in life.

He was a medic in the Great War,
wounded in the Argonne and sent home
to recover in a Hoboken hospital.
Instead of medical school, his dream,
he became a pharmacist to keep
his mother's drug store alive.
He also was a traveling salesman
to support his family in the Depression.

Our times together were special.
He took me to football games,
taught me baseball, and called me
"Daddy's man." Sunday church,
kneeling beside him at communion,
was a special time with him.

And my most painful memories?
A telephone call one rainy April day
telling us he was critically injured
in an automobile wreck while
on his second job. During four days
and nights I sat in Room 107
at a Selma hospital, watching
his broken body die. I still recall
the pattern on the linoleum floor.

Early on the morning he died,
our parish priest walked with me
to the hospital. He did not speak
but kept his arm around my shoulder.
The room was quiet, Daddy not breathing.
The drive home with my mother was
just as quiet. It was a clear spring day,
cool and without a cloud in the sky.

May 3, 1945

That Road

Somewhere along the way,
in my rush to get here from there,
I regret that I missed some things.

I did not hear wind in the elms
make the leaves talk
(but not to each other), or watch
afternoon sunlight filter through
branches of never-sleeping trees.

I took long walks in childhood
without a goal in mind,
slow days from dawn to dusk
with no need to know the time.

If only, as the moon rose,
a sly wind had gathered forces
and trees locked their winter arms
to keep me walking on that road.

Lent 2017

After Discharge From Intensive Care

You can recognize them
now that you have been there—
languid bodies, a blend
of love and loss,
with every body movement fluid
like limbs surrendered by bones.

There is no language in this limbo,
an island of monitors
and alarms that speak with a voice
foreign to those who visit
except those veteran spouses
who expect it to never end.

An island where time is measured
 only by visiting hours,
where lifeless bodies come and go
and purpose shines clear
as the world that seems to remain
outside the walls of a fortress.

Some know there will be no more
if they are lucky to have gone this far,
whatever moment they are in—
from birth's infinity to now,
distances and questions without end,
the body knows and folds the mind within.

I Wonder

For The Rev. Barbara Crafton

Will I not know that I have ceased to be
and will the soul who lived with me be free?
Nothingness could be left to fill my place
as for those who may have fallen from grace.

Or will I find the alsolife of friends
and loved ones in a world that never ends?
Bonded together forever in flight
from the unplowable prairie of night.

Aging

Of years like these,
a life is made or broken.
As we expand so does the universe.
We learn there will be even more room
when the sun dies.

Silent are evenings once filled
with music and laughter.
A voice drifts under the horizon
and grows faint—
no longer to be heard.

As we struggle against sleep
only an owl's soft cry
runs like a breath through the pines.
For a moment, the glue
joining body and soul does not ache.

Their Names

Once I was young

and the dead were in other ages.

Now how small the day is.

I see flowers appearing

in spring grass but can't remember

their names. Even the trees

have their own language.

Once the dead go

and leave behind their names,

like the spring flowers,

they go on. They never hesitate.

They go on.

The Trivial

Eighteenth century American furniture
adorns our home .When I walk into the hall
I see myself frozen in a Chippendale
mirror hung beside a grandfather clock
from New Jersey. In the dining room
stands a sideboard, Hepplewhite,
and a table with Philadelphia shield
dining room chairs, treasures cherished
and stared at by my family for years,
although my eyes wander and keep returning
to the masters of the trivial:

a smooth grey stone on the mantle
in my den brought by a great grandfather
from Wales, surrounded by stones
my son and I scooped together
on Omaha beach one November day;
a ticket stub from a Red Sox game
at Fenway; the tennis ball my daughter
used to win a state championship;
my father's box of old coins—

all valueless and forgettable detritus
my children will throw away someday
as I did my mother's diaries wrapped in string,
faded Kodak snapshots of childhood friends,
and boxes of letters from her mother Maude.

Tiny Porches

You've seen them:

cheap one-story apart-

ments

painted white

lined up a few yards

from a broken sidewalk

with tiny porches

and wooden doors

numbered 101, 102, 103…

tiny porches

with only one chair

an empty rocking chair

Thoughts on Dying

An old family doctor once said to me:
After fifty years of facing death
in my patients I have become
so acquainted with the end of life
it does not mystify or frighten me.
Each of us shall die in a unique way.
The "good death" is a myth;
death with dignity is a rare event
but the dignity of the life preceding
is what gives dignity to death.
Barring accident or tragedy,
our genes carry the answer
and our bodies tell us when it's time.

Ambassador

In the overcast, starless sky
she prevails,
sliding between the pines
until she cruises
over the dull and pouting bay.
Her priceless backpack
is filled with visions
of endless lands and caravans
after life first crawled
from some unknown wet sea.
We show her little respect,
this emissary of our galaxy.
She may bear salvation,
if such a thing exists,
or perhaps nothing at all.

Full Moon
September 6, 2017

Spring

Winter is not the season
of graves
but spring is,
when sleepers don't wake.
Then the sun
puts out
a saucer of light
we survivors lap up
like thirsty cats,
a portion
for forgetfulness
and our bickering ideas
of love and work.

We hope
we will last
for one more year
through the seasons we fear—
summer's wet heat,
fall's fever
of flaming leaves,
winter's frozen landscape.

To Pay Homage

So far gone now in my decline
what value are the lessons
I have learned to pass on
that might serve those
who follow the same road?

It is my fate to find it out—
I could have been more kind
and not broken faith
when it suited me, for now
I feel alone, the end near.

I have put my work first
all of my life and left no time
between the things achieved.
Now at times I breathe air
as if little were left there.

Vanished time has taught me
not only to list my wrongs
but to pay homage to how the years
have brought me a fitting end,
even if not the one I sought.

A Good Doctor's Advice

Take time out
to listen as your body speaks
its words to you—
words as soft as leaves
that whisper in the live oaks.

Note the attention of birds
and squirrels while they feed,
always watchful and wary,
ready to flee or fly.
Be as alert for danger as they are.

There comes a subtle shift
in eyes, in skin, the bones within,
in muscles thin and wasting
with the unknown time that's left.
Your bones and blood will speak
to you as they move,
 like the cells of your skin
as they wither and cannot mend.
If you are lucky to have gone so far.
you will not pass this way again.

And your dreams—
listen to what they yearn to tell you
of the secrets you have hidden
in your mind as it sleeps.
Let them awaken and give you hope,
let them guide you to safe harbor.

September 4, 2017

Winds of Fall

Oak leaves depart
with the winds of fall,
an abrupt farewell
to spring's essence,
summer's rich foliage,
the company of the living.

They now shrug off
their fallen fate
as if they'd never lived
in the green vegetation
of the undead,
as they drift to a ground
hardened by frost.

Don't act surprised,
you faded beauties,
as you toss about
in the chilling wind
on your bed of mortality.
You knew all along
you'd be mulched
into the void of winter
like stars that die
before they know
they're gone.

You Can't Go Home Again

Despite Thomas Wolfe's advice,
I went home again.
Parents and friends were gone,
but the homestead was standing.

Old servants began to appear
when they saw me there,
each anxious to tell me
how life *was*—back in the forties.

My father loved maples in October
and preferred his steak rare.
My mother never served us
lamb on Sunday without mint jelly,

never went to church without
hat and gloves, and so on.
Even neighbors I had forgotten
emerged slowly from old houses.

They still clung to memories
and, maybe, to the sense of loss they bring.
That day—from endless mouths—
my dead assembled.

Uniontown, Alabama
circa 1970

93

Christmas in Paris

It was dry before the rain.
Pigeons shifted together,
black as their shadows.
Flags whipped the sky clean.

Cold had wrapped its hands
around the throat of winter.
It raked our bodies
like a knife on plane glass

and sliced a winter pattern
on our faces.
It watched the wind twist
and bend the cypress.

It listened to voices
pouring from the rain.
It sharpened itself
on the wind's whetstone

and left its mark,
freshly carved
and still bleeding
on a wet mare's traces.

What Some Grownups Remember

Some grownups remember Christmas
when childhood moments surface
in those quiet and empty rooms
where once parents, long dead,
struggled to bring them joyful surprise.

In the blur of work, food, sleep
they sigh such platitudes:
We have our health. We have
each other and financial security.
Yet they know that even these gifts
 can be snatched away as if
  they were children wanting too much.

Better to be content as in childhood
when they found joy in a stocking
hung on the mantelpiece
beside their Christmas tree,
a stocking filled with:
    peppermint sticks,
  Juicy Fruit chewing gum,
   and Mars candy bars.

Christmas 2017

A Solstitial Winter Day

Outside this window, clear and cold,

a pale and shallow graying sun

awaits the planet's tilt to winter

and the shortest light of day.

As the moon rises above the hill

a wily wind gathers forces,

and trees, in their black silhouettes,

link their winter arms.

Winter Solstice
December 21, 2017

On the Shortest Day

In the shortest light of day

the moon rises above the hill

and a sly wind gathers forces—

a wind of memories blows

through this body—

people, places, and names.

In it burns the pain

of worn-out bones, lost friends.

This body then tilts

as Earth, the planet, spins

and returns beneath

the spinning planet's wings

Winter Solstice 2017

A Blanket of Leaves

The house empty, he sleeps.
Faces drift toward him
like showers of leaves,
one, his father—
that face a map of the world
seen from a great height.

He questions: *Do you know now*
what we seek to know?
And then he asks:
The dead, where aren't they?
He ponders: *If there is anything*
to know, my father must know it.

But his questions unanswered,
he could only wonder:
Do the dead know all, or just
what's in their neighborhood?
Eyes closed, he sleeps
under a blanket of leaves.

Plumbobbing

Gus, my best friend, created the word
when we were med students
struggling with physical diagnosis
and the art of auscultation
of the heart and lungs.

Instead of having his patients
remove or open their shirts or gowns
he would slide his stethoscope
under their top garments
and listen intently as they breathed.

Of course he never did this
when instructors or visiting staff
were present and when asked
about this maneuver he would say:
"I'm plumbobbing the patient."

He became a radiologist,
perhaps reflecting his disinterest
in bedside skills, and practiced
the art of reading shadows
until he died at seventy-five.

I can imagine him now
in a new life as a bedside clinician,
carefully examining patients,
surrounded by admirers who watch
as he skillfully plumbobs each patient.

What We Know

We will all die someday,
said the hospital chaplain
to a pancreatic cancer patient,
a sergeant to his men on Omaha beach,
a Twin Tower window mate on 9/11,
the next in line at Dachau,
Hitler to Eva Braun in the bunker,
and, yes, the captain of the Titanic.

Death is relentless and yet so subtle
to the innocent who do not know
its disregard for youth, fame, or failure.
Merciless on the pediatric ward
and unpredictable elsewhere,
it sits in the corner of every room
wearing the same clothes,
indifferent to every one.

Godparents

They come to look at a baby's face
whose eyes cannot see the godparents
standing by the font of holy water
in various seasons of aging.

They had stopped going to funerals
once they knew the dead from childhood,
and weddings when broken covenants
were repeated with a smile.

So they come to baptisms
even though they must recite again
the ten commandments, all of them broken
except the one about murder.

Time gives them a moment—
to sense and smell the innocence of youth,
to feel washed clean and new in spirit—
then snatches it back again.

A Grandfather's Request

Give funerals a new face—
one not to haunt children
long after flowers are dead
in the mourning parlor.
Let there be no guest books,
homemade pies, and casseroles.

Do not hire a black hearse
or usher in the grief walkers.
Forget tents and folding chairs,
caravans of creeping cars
with tinted windows.

Open the shutters,
play waltzes on the Victrola.
Go past crowded graveyards,
visit a favorite place.
Walk together in sun or rain,
carry the urn in your hands.

Unborn Words

What happened to them,

the words never spoken

or written, pleaded, or chanted?

Are they flying somewhere

on the wings of swallows,

or are they planted

like seeds in fertile fields,

hoping to be picked

like new flowers

to grow and live again

in searching minds?

Perhaps they have joined

all beings gone extinct

and are lost forever

in unspoken nothingness.

Moments

When they ask
how your life is doing,
do you think of worry
and fear mixed with moments
of joy and hope?

Moments that are ordinary,
lonely, extraordinary,
all saved from childhood
as what is learned,
and seem so important
until they all fall
into the abyss of age?

Yet there is always something
worse, and something better,
as we slowly break apart—
moments so intense
it seems they are eternal.
Perhaps they are.

Easter 2018

Our Broken World

For The Rev. Michael Hoffman

We live in a broken world
of human suffering—
natural disasters, epidemics,
and wars to name a few—
none of them God's will.

Evil and the sins of man
were born when freedom of will
was abused by greed.
No one is spared
the grief of human suffering.

Yet God is always there
when we feel alone in the wilderness,
always with us in our broken world,
calling to us to help Him
put it together again.

Lent 2018

Title Index

TITLE INDEX

All of Henry Langhorne's books, except for *Tombigbee*, *Listen to the River*, and *Winter Clothes*, are available at amazon.com.

In Search of Solitude is also available online from Barnes & Noble and other major outlets.

All of the books, except for *Listen to the River*, which is out of print, are also available from the publisher.

Pelican Press Pensacola
Pensacola, FL 32514
850-206-4608
pelican.post@att.net
www.pelicanpresspensacola.com

About the Author

Henry Langhorne, former Poet Laureate of Northwest Florida (1999-2009), is the author of eleven collections of poetry. He is currently a member of the Academy of American Poets.

For over twenty years, Henry Langhorne's poems have been published in a number of local and regional periodicals, including: *The Sewanee Review (Winter 2016), Hurricane Review, The Panhandler, Emerald Coast Review, Negative Capability, Poem, The Cape Rock, The Chattahoochee Review, Plainsongs, Passager, Inlet, Mediphors, Life on the Line* (anthology), *Dockside, On Wings of Spirit* (anthology), *The Pharos*, and the *Journal of the American Medical Association* (JAMA).

His boyhood home was in Uniontown, Alabama, a small town in a stretch of rich, black earth known as the Black Belt, a part of the Canebrake from which *The Canebrake Collection* got its title. This fertile cotton land was near the Tombigbee River where tall stands of canebrake once grew.

Henry Langhorne attended undergraduate school at The University of the South at Sewanee, followed by graduation from Tulane Medical School in 1957. He served his internship at Charity Hospital in New Orleans, where he also obtained specialty training. Later, he became the oldest ever graduate student at Sewanee when he earned his Master of Fine Arts (MFA) degree in Creative Writing in May of 2016.

Henry Langhorne retired in December of 2014 as the senior member of Cardiology Consultants, after practicing cardiology in Pensacola, Florida, since 1963.

www.ingramcontent.com/pod-product-compliance
Lightning Source LLC
Chambersburg PA
CBHW020914090426
42736CB00008B/634